I0453637

L.S. SMITH

Screw Up Like A Genius

How To Fail Better, Break the Rules, and Win at Being Human

WINK & WORD
PUBLISHING

First published by Wink & Word Publishing 2025

Copyright © 2025 by L.S. Smith

All rights reserved. No part of this publication may be reproduced, stored or transmitted in any form or by any means, electronic, mechanical, photocopying, recording, scanning, or otherwise without written permission from the publisher. It is illegal to copy this book, post it to a website, or distribute it by any other means without permission.

This novel is entirely a work of fiction. The names, characters and incidents portrayed in it are the work of the author's imagination. Any resemblance to actual persons, living or dead, events or localities is entirely coincidental.

First edition

This book was professionally typeset on Reedsy.
Find out more at reedsy.com

For the perfectionists, procrastinators, and professional overthinkers—
may you finally laugh at your chaos, forgive your past,
and love the brilliantly flawed masterpiece that is you.

"Perfection never taught me anything useful. My best lessons showed up wearing chaos and coffee stains."

L.S. Smith

Contents

Introduction

A Permission Slip to Be Human

If you've ever tripped over nothing, burned toast while "multitasking," or cried because your Wi-Fi dropped during a deep, emotional episode of your favorite show—welcome. You belong here.

This is not another "fix your life" manual written by someone who color-codes their sock drawer. This is a *permission slip to be human.* To screw up, show up, and laugh through the in-between parts where most people edit their highlight reels.

Here's the truth: life is not an inspirational quote on a sunset background. It's a series of weird experiments involving caffeine, stubborn hope, and an unreasonable amount of self-doubt. But that's okay—because the goal isn't to be perfect. It's to be present.

I've learned that perfection doesn't create peace—it just breeds panic. The constant fear of failing, of being judged, of not being enough... it's exhausting. So I stopped chasing perfect and started chasing *possible.* Sometimes that means dropping the ball and juggling it anyway. Sometimes it means laughing at my own disasters before they turn into stories I can tell later.

This book is for the people who secretly wonder if they're the only ones pretending to know what they're doing (you're not). It's for the ones carrying guilt over mistakes that happened three jobs, two relationships, or fifteen years ago (you can set that down now). It's for anyone who wants to stop surviving and start living—imperfectly, hilariously, wholeheartedly.

You don't need to have it all together to be a masterpiece. You just need to remember that even when life looks like a mess, it's still art in progress.

So take a deep breath, put down the unrealistic expectations, and grab your metaphorical glue gun.

We're going to laugh, cry, and build something beautifully imperfect together.

Welcome to *Screw Up Like a Genius.*

1

Fail Like You Mean It

Let's get one thing straight: failure is not the enemy.

Failure is that brutally honest friend who tells you the truth while handing you a glass of wine.

We spend our entire lives trying to dodge it, outsmart it, or bury it under perfectly filtered success stories. But here's the thing—no one escapes unscathed. Not the overachievers, not the Zen yogis, not even that one guy from high school who somehow became a motivational speaker.

Everyone fails. The only difference is that some of us learn to *fail with style.*

The Art of Failing Publicly (and Living to Tell About It)

I once tried to impress a room full of professionals by giving a big, polished presentation. I rehearsed every line, printed color-coded charts, and even wore shoes that looked responsible. Five minutes in, my slideshow froze, I panicked, and—because the universe loves good comedy—I accidentally hit the button that displayed my *personal grocery list* instead.

There it was, projected in 4K glory: "Toilet paper, red wine, cookie dough, and dry shampoo."

For a split second, I wanted to vanish. But then… I laughed. Out loud.

And so did everyone else.

That day taught me something: people don't connect with perfection. They connect with *humanness.* My little moment of public disaster made me more relatable than any perfectly memorized speech ever could.

It's a reminder we all need sometimes: failing doesn't make you unworthy. It makes you *understandable and human.*

Failure Is Proof You're Participating

We treat failure like it's radioactive—something to avoid at all costs. But here's the truth: *the only people who never fail are the ones who never try.*

Failure means you showed up. You risked something. You cared enough to step out of your comfort zone instead of clinging to the illusion of safety.

The greatest irony? Most people spend their lives fearing failure while living in quiet failure every day—stuck, scared, and waiting for perfect conditions that never come.

Perfection is procrastination in a shiny outfit.

And the sooner you stop waiting for perfect, the sooner you start *living.*

The Myth of "Doing It Right"

We were raised to believe there's a right way to do life. The right job, the right marriage, the right house with the right countertops and the right photo of your smiling family framed on the right wall.

And if you deviate from the script, society looks at you like you're the cautionary tale.

But have you ever met someone who actually followed "the right path" and ended up genuinely fulfilled? They're rare. Because "right" is usually just code for "what makes everyone else comfortable."

There's no right way to live. There's only *your* way.

The way that includes mistakes, restarts, detours, and days where you eat cereal for dinner and call it a win.

When you stop trying to do life "right," you finally start doing it *real*.

Your Brain Is a Drama Queen (or King)

Let's talk about why we fear failure so much.

Our brains are wired for survival, not happiness. Back in caveman days, failing could literally get you eaten by a tiger. Today, the tiger is just your boss, your mother-in-law, or that voice in your head whispering, "What if everyone thinks you're ridiculous?"

News flash: everyone already thinks about themselves too much to care about your minor disasters.

But your brain doesn't know that. It thinks you're still one mistake away from social extinction.

So it plays out disaster scenarios: *If I fail this interview, I'll never get another job. If I mess up this date, I'll die alone with twelve cats.*

Meanwhile, reality is far kinder.

You fail. You learn. You laugh. You get up.

Repeat until legend status is achieved.

Fail Like You Mean It

If you're going to fail—and you are—do it on purpose.

Not because you want to fail, but because you're no longer afraid of it.

Fail like you mean it.

Put your whole, brilliant, imperfect self into something even if it might fall apart.

Apply for the job. Start the business. Write the book. Ask the person out. Try the salsa class even if you have the rhythm of a confused toddler.

Stop tiptoeing around life trying to avoid embarrassment. You're already embarrassing. We all are. The sooner you accept that, the freer you become.

Failure: The Great Equalizer

No one's immune. Not your boss, not your therapist, not even that influencer who swears her "morning routine changed her life" (because she filmed it in good lighting, not in real life).

Everyone you admire has a trail of spectacular faceplants behind them. They just stopped calling them failures — and started calling them *chapters.*

Think about it: failure is the most universal human experience. You don't need a passport, degree, or matching set of luggage to experience it. You just need to try something.

And yet, we act like failure is shameful — when in reality, it's *the only thing that makes us relatable.*

People don't bond over perfection. They bond over, "Oh my God, that happened to you too?"

The Perfection Hangover

Perfectionism is just fear dressed up in a power suit.

It tells you that if you do everything right, you'll finally feel safe, loved, respected.

Spoiler: you won't.

Because perfection is an illusion — a moving target that gets farther away the harder you chase it. You could spend your whole life trying to meet standards no one else is actually enforcing but you.

Meanwhile, life is over there waving, saying, "Hey! You can actually enjoy me anytime now."

The real cost of perfection isn't just exhaustion — it's missing your life while trying to edit it.

The Emotional Side of Falling Flat

Let's be honest — failure hurts. It bruises the ego and scrapes the heart.

You try something with hope and heart, and when it collapses, it stings.

But you know what's worse than falling? Standing perfectly still because you're afraid to try.

Every stumble teaches you something stillness never will.

Failure isn't final. It's feedback.

You didn't fail at love — you learned how you deserve to be treated.

You didn't fail at a dream — you learned how to build one that fits you better.

You didn't fail at being perfect — you learned you're human.

And that's the whole point.

The Gift of Laughing at Yourself

Humor doesn't erase pain; it helps you carry it.

When you can laugh at your mistakes, they lose their power over you.

They become part of your story instead of the reason you stopped telling it.

The most magnetic people aren't the ones who have it all figured out — they're the ones who can say, "Yep, that was a disaster," and grin about it.

Laughter is the language of resilience.

It's how we trick our fear into standing down long enough to move forward.

So yes, laugh when you spill your coffee, say the wrong name in a meeting, or forget why you walked into a room.

You're not broken — you're just living in HD.

Fail Forward, Not Forever

There's a difference between failing and *becoming* a failure.

Failing is what happens; "failure" is the story you tell yourself about it.

When you screw up, it's not a full stop — it's a comma.

Take a breath. Reflect. Adjust. Keep writing your story.

Every success you've ever seen was built on the rubble of things that didn't work out. Every inventor, artist, and leader you've ever admired has a private museum of bad ideas, rejections, and spectacularly awkward attempts.

The secret? They didn't stop. They failed *forward*.

The Permission to Begin Again

You've already failed before — and guess what? You're still here.

That means you're resilient. Stubborn. Brave enough to keep trying even when it's hard.

That's not weakness. That's genius.

Failing like you mean it doesn't mean you love failure — it means you love yourself enough to keep showing up after it.

To try again with softer expectations, louder laughter, and a little more grace for the person in the mirror.

Every time you rise after falling, you reinforce the truth that's been waiting for you all along:

You were never meant to be flawless. You were meant to be *free*.

Your Takeaway

You don't need to avoid failure — you need to invite it to dinner, pour it a drink, and ask what it's trying to teach you.

Fail like you mean it.

Fall forward with purpose.

Laugh loudly at your mistakes.

And then, for the love of all things human, keep going. Because the only real failure is never finding out what could've happened if you had just tried.

2

The Cult of Perfectionism

How to Break Up with the Illusion of Having It All Together

There's a very specific sound that perfectionists make when life doesn't go their way. It's somewhere between a sigh, a silent scream, and the noise you make when you stub your toe in public but don't want anyone to know.

If that sound feels familiar, congratulations — you might be a member of The Cult of Perfectionism.

The good news? Membership is free. The bad news? The dues are your peace of mind.

The Church of "Should"

Perfectionism has its own religion — and its favorite word is *should.*

You should be more productive.

You should be happier.

You should eat better, exercise more, meditate daily, love your job, and wake up every morning with gratitude and abs.

Perfectionism preaches that if you just "try harder," you'll finally achieve inner peace. But peace doesn't come from control — it comes from *acceptance.* And perfectionists are allergic to acceptance.

We think if we can just fix everything — the house, the face, the relationship, the résumé — we'll finally earn the right to rest.

Except perfection doesn't lead to rest. It leads to *restlessness.*

Because perfection is a finish line that keeps moving every time you get close.

Confessions of a Recovering Perfectionist

I used to be fluent in perfection. My planner was color-coded, my closet organized by emotional stability level, and I had a nervous breakdown every time someone noticed I was human.

If I forgot to send an email, I'd replay it in my head for days.

If someone didn't text back, I'd assume they secretly hated me.

And don't even get me started on hosting — I once cleaned my house *before* the cleaning service arrived because God forbid they knew how I actually lived.

I wasn't chasing excellence; I was sprinting from shame.

Perfectionism looks like ambition from the outside, but from the inside, it's just anxiety wearing mascara.

How We Got Here

It's not entirely our fault. We were raised in a world that graded us on performance, not presence.

From childhood, we learned that gold stars, trophies, and approval meant safety. We were praised for getting it right, not for being brave enough to try.

So we grew up believing that love and worth were things we earned by being impressive. And now we're adults who panic if our living rooms look "lived in."

Our society worships polished surfaces — curated feeds, filtered selfies, motivational quotes about "crushing it."

Meanwhile, we're quietly crumbling under the weight of pretending to have it all together.

The Psychology of Perfect

Let's get scientific for a second. Perfectionism isn't a personality trait — it's a coping mechanism.

At its root, perfectionism says: *If I'm flawless, no one can reject me.*

It's armor disguised as achievement.

But armor is heavy. It keeps people at a distance. You can't receive love or connection when you're too busy managing your image.

Perfectionism whispers, "Once you're better, thinner, richer, calmer, smarter — *then* you'll be worthy."

But worthiness isn't a reward. It's a birthright.

You don't have to hustle for it. You don't have to earn it. You just have to remember it.

Signs You Might Be a Perfectionist (Even If You Deny It)

Let's play a quick game. If you laugh (or wince) at any of these, you might be one of us:

- You rewrite texts three times so they sound "casual but intelligent."
- You have 43 drafts in your email because you're afraid of sounding "too much."
- You rehearse arguments in your head like a one-person Broadway show.
- You can't start a project until you've researched every possible mistake you *might* make.
- You delete photos that show pores, wrinkles, or a chair out of place.
- You say, "It's fine" when it's definitely not fine.
- You feel guilty when you rest because "you could be doing something productive."

If you nodded to at least two of those... welcome, my friend. You are beautifully, hilariously human.

The Cost of Chasing Perfect

The pursuit of perfection might make your Instagram grid look fantastic, but it's murder on your mental health.

It's not just stress — it's exhaustion disguised as discipline.

You start every day already behind, measuring yourself against an impossible ideal that doesn't actually exist.

Perfectionists live in a constant state of "almost."

Almost good enough. Almost ready. Almost there.

And "almost" is a miserable place to live.

It steals your joy. It numbs your creativity. It convinces you that every mistake is proof you're not worthy — instead of proof you're *alive*.

We tell ourselves, "I'll relax when everything's done." But everything is *never* done. Life keeps moving the goalpost.

And one day, you realize you spent years waiting for permission to feel good about yourself.

Perfection's Cruelest Trick

The cruelest trick perfectionism plays is convincing you that it's protecting you — when really, it's preventing you.

It keeps you safe, sure, but safe is not the same as fulfilled.

You can't create, love, or grow without risk. You can't experience joy without vulnerability.

Trying to be perfect is like trying to hold your breath while running a marathon. You can't perform and breathe at the same time. Eventually, something gives.

The Moment I Let Go

When I turned 50, something strange happened — I stopped caring so much.

Not in a bitter, "get off my lawn" kind of way, but in a peaceful, *"you know what, I've earned the right to wear stretchy pants to brunch"* kind of way.

There was no big party, no fireworks, no life-changing trip to Bali where I found myself between smoothie bowls. Just me, a cup of coffee strong enough to wake the dead, and the quiet realization that I'd spent far too many years trying to be the "best version" of myself.

At 50, I decided I just wanted to be the *real* version — the one who forgets what she walked into a room for but still remembers to laugh about it.

I looked around my kitchen — at the mismatched mugs, the mail I meant to sort three days ago, the plant I was definitely neglecting — and felt this wave of calm. I didn't need to fix everything. I just needed to live in it.

So I poured another cup of coffee, raised it like a toast, and said out loud, "You're doing fine, kid."

Then I added, "Now maybe water the plant before it files for emancipation."

And that was it. No dramatic revelation. No angels singing. Just peace, laughter, and the kind of freedom that comes when you finally stop auditioning for your own life.

And it felt good. It felt *real.*

Because "real" is magnetic in a world obsessed with manufactured.

Breaking the Spell

So how do we escape The Cult of Perfectionism?

You don't need a dramatic exit — just small acts of rebellion.

- Post the photo even if your hair is weird.
- Send the email even if it's not Pulitzer-worthy.
- Rest without earning it.
- Laugh when things fall apart.
- Let "good enough" be your new mantra.

Every time you choose real over perfect, you break the spell a little more.

Reframing the Fear

Instead of asking, "What if I fail?"

Start asking, "What if I don't?"

What if the thing you're scared of doing badly becomes the thing that changes your life?

What if the imperfections are the very parts that make you unforgettable?

You are not here to be flawless. You're here to be *felt.*

And no one feels perfection — they feel presence.

A New Definition of Success

Success isn't never messing up.

It's being brave enough to keep showing up — messy hair, coffee stains, and all.

It's learning to be proud of yourself for *trying,* not just for triumphing.

It's knowing you can be both a masterpiece and a work in progress at the same time.

Perfect isn't the goal anymore. Peace is.

Peace with your quirks. Peace with your pace. Peace with the fact that you're a gloriously unfinished project.

Your Takeaway

Perfectionism will whisper, "You'll be happy when…"

But happiness doesn't wait for when. It happens *while.*

You don't need to impress anyone.

You don't need to earn your worth.

You don't need to hold it all together.

You just need to let go — and trust that who you are, right now, is enough.

Because the truth is simple- Perfect is boring. *Real* is unforgettable

3

Comparisonitis Is a Hell of a Drug

Why Everyone Else's Highlight Reel Is Not Your Measuring Stick

The Scroll Spiral

It always starts innocently.

You're just going to check one thing on social media — maybe a friend's vacation photo or that recipe reel you saved three months ago. Five minutes later, you're 47 posts deep into someone's cousin's engagement in Santorini, staring at a sunset that looks Photoshopped by God Himself.

You glance around your own living room. The lighting isn't romantic; it's fluorescent. The only thing sparkling is the dog's water bowl, and your dinner is a bowl of cereal because you didn't have the energy to "assemble" food tonight.

Suddenly, your perfectly fine life feels… inadequate.

That's the thing about comparisonitis — it's a gateway drug. One scroll and you're high on the illusion that everyone else has it figured out. Their relationships are thriving, their skin glows, their children are cooperative, and their sourdough has a better rise than your self-esteem.

Meanwhile, you're sitting there in a T-shirt that says *"Probably Late for Something,"* wondering if you missed some secret class in adulthood where they handed out grace, balance, and matching furniture.

The Comparison Hangover

Comparison gives you a temporary buzz — that little shot of envy-laced adrenaline — but it always ends the same way: with a hangover of self-doubt and disappointment.

You close the app, but it's too late. Your brain's already spiraling.

You're suddenly convinced you should be doing more, earning more, loving better, aging slower, and meditating faster.

You start measuring your behind-the-scenes against everyone else's highlight reel, forgetting that what you're seeing online is 10% reality, 90% ring light.

The truth is, no one's life looks as good as it does online — not even the people who post it.

The mom or dad with the color-coordinated snacks cried in their car this morning.

The couple posting romantic beach photos argued over sunscreen ten minutes before.

And the woman whose "effortless" morning routine includes yoga, journaling, and lemon water? She probably hit snooze three times and bribed her dog to take that serene photo.

We're all performing, to some degree. The tragedy is that we compare our raw footage to everyone else's edited trailer.

Your Brain's Got Trust Issues

Our brains have one job: keep us alive. But in the modern world, they've turned that survival instinct into a neurotic side hustle.

Once upon a time, comparison kept us safe. We compared ourselves to others in our tribe to figure out our role — who hunted best, who gathered, who told stories. It was social calibration, not competition.

Now? Our "tribe" is eight billion people, and our brain still thinks their success means we're in danger of being left behind on the proverbial tundra.

That's why you can logically *know* that someone else's happiness doesn't threaten yours — but emotionally, it feels like losing a race you never agreed to run.

Comparison isn't about jealousy; it's about fear. Fear that we're not enough, that we're missing out, that we're failing some invisible test everyone else seems to be passing.

Behind the Filters

Here's the truth no one posts about: every perfect photo has a pile of laundry just outside the frame.

We curate our lives like art exhibits. We show the clean corners, the smiling faces, the "I woke up like this" selfies that took seventeen tries.

Meanwhile, behind the scenes, everyone's juggling the same chaos — bills, insecurities, overcooked dinners, and the occasional emotional breakdown in a parking lot.

We all have both the highlight reel *and* the blooper reel. It's just that most of us only share one.

And honestly, that's fine — people don't owe us their pain.

But we owe *ourselves* the truth: no one is as calm, confident, or collected as they appear. Everyone's just improvising. Some are just better at filters.

How It Sneaks Into Everything

Comparison doesn't just live online. It hides everywhere.

In friendships — when your friend's life seems to be moving faster than yours.

In parenting — when someone's kid gets into the gifted program while yours gets into your makeup drawer.

In careers — when you start to feel like success skipped your address.

Even in healing — because yes, some people manage to make self-care look competitive-your friend says to you *"Oh wow, You're still journaling? I've moved on to gratitude vision boarding."*

Comparison is sneaky like that. It shapeshifts into every part of life until you start measuring your worth by invisible rulers.

The Exhaustion of Measuring

The problem with constantly comparing yourself is that it keeps you distracted from your actual life.

You stop noticing your own progress because you're too busy watching someone else's.

You forget that the person you're envying has probably envied someone else — maybe even you.

We're all stuck in the same ridiculous loop of trying to outdo one another at being content.

It's like everyone's on stage performing "I'm Fine: The Musical," and the audience is just other actors pretending to enjoy the show.

The Truth About "Enough"

"Enough" is a moving target.

You think once you reach it, you'll feel satisfied. But once you get there, your brain immediately resets the bar higher.

It's not that you're broken. It's that you've been trained to chase worth instead of recognize it.

When you constantly measure your life against someone else's, you lose sight of how far you've already come. You forget that the version of you from five years ago would be *amazed* at what you've survived, built, and become.

Enough isn't a destination. It's a decision.

How to Detox from Comparisonitis

Here's the good news: this addiction is curable. And the withdrawal symptoms are mostly laughter and peace.

Start with these small but mighty steps:

Name It When It Happens.
When you catch yourself scrolling and spiraling, say out loud, "This is a highlight reel." It snaps your brain back to reality.

Trade Consumption for Creation.
Every minute you spend comparing could be spent creating something that's actually yours — a meal, a walk, a doodle, a thought.

Gratitude Is the Antidote.
Nothing kills comparison faster than noticing what you already have. You can't be grateful and envious at the same time.

Set Boundaries with Your Feed.
If someone's posts make you feel like you're perpetually losing, mute them. Protect your peace like it's on the endangered species list.

Celebrate, Don't Compete.
When you see someone succeeding, let it be proof that good things are possible — not proof that you're behind.

Remember: You're the Main Character of Your Own Story.
You're not a background extra in someone else's plotline. You're the star of your messy, hilarious, perfectly imperfect life.

The Beauty of Staying in Your Lane

You can't run your race while watching someone else's track.

And you'll never reach your joy if you keep rerouting yourself toward someone else's finish line.

The goal isn't to be better than anyone. It's to be better than yesterday.

To wake up each day with just enough self-respect to try again, even if no one's watching.

When you stop comparing, you start noticing.

You see the little things again — the way your coffee smells, the song that always lifts your mood, the small moments that make up a real, beautiful life.

That's where happiness hides — in the unshared, unfiltered moments that don't need validation to matter.

The Takeaway

Comparison is a thief, but only if you leave the door open.

You don't need to measure up. You just need to *show up.*

For your own story, your own pace, your own joy.

Your life isn't late. It's just unfolding on schedule — your schedule.

And when you stop trying to match someone else's timing, you finally start living in your own rhythm.

So, unfollow the myth that you're behind.

The only person you need to compete with is the one you were yesterday — **and you'll be proud of how far you've come.**

4

Why "Having It All Together" Is a Lie

And Why Falling Apart Might Be the Best Thing That Ever Happened to You

The Together Myth

You know those people who seem to have their lives completely together?

The ones who somehow manage to work full-time, meal-prep quinoa, never forget a birthday, and still have the energy to post sunrise selfies with motivational captions like *"Grind. Glow. Grow."*

Yeah. They're lying.

Okay, maybe not lying exactly — but they're definitely editing. Because no one, and I mean no one, has it all together. Not even the ones who color-code their calendars and own matching storage bins.

For every "put-together" moment you see, there's a messy counterbalance happening off-screen — the unwashed coffee mug, the email they forgot to send, the minor existential crisis in the Target parking lot.

Behind every curated image of order is a person just trying to make sense of the chaos — sometimes succeeding, often improvising, and always wondering if it shows.

Where the Lie Began

Somewhere along the line, "having it all together" became the ultimate life goal — like we were supposed to unlock some magical stage of adulthood where laundry folds itself and emotions stay politely in their lanes.

Blame it on sitcoms, social media, or that one relentlessly cheerful coworker who shows up at 8 a.m. with fresh blow-dried hair and a homemade kale muffin. Somewhere we confused *competence* with *control* — and control with happiness.

We started believing that success meant never dropping a ball, never losing our temper, never being seen without eyeliner or enthusiasm.

But the truth? The people who look like they have it all together are usually the ones who've just learned how to hide their unraveling better than the rest of us.

The Secret Everyone's Keeping

Here's a little secret no one tells you: everyone's juggling something.

The coworker who's "always positive"? She cries in the shower sometimes.

The dad who seems chill about everything? He's quietly terrified he's screwing it all up.

The couple who posts constant romantic date nights? They argued over where to park five minutes before the photo.

Everyone has a backstory. Everyone's carrying invisible things — anxiety, grief, guilt, overwhelm, or just plain old exhaustion.

The illusion of "having it all together" is held up by duct tape and caffeine. And that's okay. Because maybe we're not supposed to hold it all together. Maybe we're supposed to *hold each other* instead.

The Performance Trap

We're experts at pretending.

"Everything's fine!" we chirp, even when it's clearly not.

We post smiling photos after tear-stained mornings. We show up to work when our hearts are somewhere else. We tell people "I'm good" because it's easier than admitting we're tired of being good all the time.

It's emotional theater — the performance of composure.

But here's the problem: *pretending to be okay doesn't make you okay. It just makes you lonely.*

When you fake fine, you block the connection that could actually make things better. Real strength isn't keeping it together — it's being honest enough to say, "I'm falling apart a little today, but I'm still here."

Falling Apart Gracefully (and Sometimes Hilariously)

Let's be real: life has no respect for your schedule.

It will serve you chaos in the middle of your "calm era" just to see how you react.

You'll spill coffee on the one white outfit you own, your phone will die right before you need directions, and your dog will choose *that* moment to roll in something mysterious and wet.

Falling apart is inevitable. Doing it gracefully is optional.

Personally, I recommend doing it with humor.

Laughing through the mess doesn't mean you don't care — it means you've accepted that control is overrated. Sometimes the most spiritual thing you can do is mutter "of course this happened" and keep going.

When My "Together" Fell Apart

For most of my life, I believed that if I worked hard enough, stayed kind enough, and kept everything neatly labeled in emotional Tupperware, I could hold it all together.

Then it happened…my divorce — and with it, the glorious unraveling of my "holding it together" illusion.

There's something surreal about watching the life you built start to come apart in slow motion.

You keep trying to tidy it up — like maybe if you just fold the laundry, keep a perfect household and pay the bills on time, you can trick the universe into giving you extra credit for effort.

But heartbreak doesn't care how organized your calendar is.

In the beginning, I tried to *manage* my pain like a project. I read articles titled "How to Thrive After Divorce" and made lists of things I was going to do: learn Italian, take up yoga, get really into self help and lose weight.

You know what I actually did?

I cried, laughed at my own crying, binged every comforting show I could find, and ordered tacos and Chinese food at midnight because I could.

One night, I was sitting alone at my kitchen table surrounded by takeout containers, work, and half a bottle of red wine — and I started to laugh. Not the polite, social kind of laugh, but the "Oh my God, this is my life now" kind.

And in that moment, I realized something I hadn't felt in a long time: *freedom.*

Because as painful as it was, the end of that marriage forced me to let go — not just of someone else, but of the version of myself who thought she could hold everything together forever.

It was messy, it was loud, and it was honest.

And somewhere between the tears and the laughter, I started to feel… real again.

I learned that falling apart isn't failure. It's an invitation — to rebuild differently, more truthfully, with more room to breathe.

My "together" didn't survive the divorce, but *I* did.

And honestly? I like this version of me better. She's softer, funnier, and finally done pretending to have all the answers.

The Real Definition of "Together"

Together isn't about perfection — it's about alignment.

It's not about polished schedules or spotless homes; it's about knowing who you are and what matters most.

Having it together means showing up — even when you're frazzled, late, or emotionally out of breath.

It means asking for help instead of pretending you don't need it.

It means being kind to yourself when everything's messy, because life doesn't reward you for suffering quietly.

You can be strong and uncertain. Brave and exhausted. Whole and healing at the same time.

The goal isn't to look like you've got it together — it's to *feel at peace with not always having it together.*

Letting People See the Real You

The scariest — and most freeing — thing you can do is let people see you as you are.

It's counterintuitive, right? We think vulnerability will make people pull away, but it actually draws them closer.

When you drop the act, you give everyone around you permission to exhale, too.

We don't need more polished people. We need more honest ones.

The kind who admit, "I'm trying my best," and mean it.

The kind who know that having a soft heart in a hard world is its own kind of victory.

The Beauty of Unraveling

Maybe "together" was never the goal.

Maybe the beauty is in the unraveling — in the becoming.

When things fall apart, it's usually because they're making space for something real.

Falling apart forces you to drop what isn't working, to rebuild stronger, freer, and less interested in impressing anyone.

Sometimes the universe has to knock your color-coded planner right off the table to remind you: life isn't meant to be managed. It's meant to be lived.

The Takeaway

No one has it all together.

Everyone's winging it — some just accessorize better.

You don't need to chase "together." You need to chase truth.

The truth that you're allowed to be a masterpiece and a work in progress at the same time.

That strength isn't the absence of struggle — it's the courage to laugh through it.

So stop trying to hold it all together.

Let it wobble. Let it breathe. Let it be gloriously human.

5

The Beauty of Being a Glorious Disaster

Hot Mess Energy

There's a special kind of magic that happens when you finally stop pretending to have it all together.

One day, you spill coffee on your shirt before a meeting, forget where you put your keys (again), and realize halfway through the day that your eyeliner's been doing its own thing since 9 a.m.

And instead of melting down, you just… laugh.

You shrug, take a sip of your lukewarm coffee, and think, *"Honestly, this tracks for my life."*

That's Hot Mess Energy — not the reckless, chaotic kind that ends in regret, but the grounded, funny, self-aware kind that says, "I'm human, and I'm done auditioning for flawless."

Because honestly? Life's more fun when you stop trying to be a masterpiece and start enjoying being a work in progress.

The Myth of the Polished Life

We've been sold a lie — that happiness comes wrapped in linen napkins and good lighting.

From the time we're little, we're told to be "neat," "quiet," "put-together." Don't make waves. Don't make noise. And for heaven's sake, don't make a mess.

But the truth is, the mess *is* where life happens.

The kitchen disasters, the failed attempts, the moments where you're laughing so hard you snort — those are the ones you'll remember.

No one looks back and gets misty-eyed over perfectly folded towels. They remember the night the power went out and you lit candles, ordered pizza, and laughed until your sides hurt.

Sure… polished is pretty. But real is *unforgettable*.

Embracing the Glorious Disaster Within

Somewhere along the way, we decided that "being put together" was the goal — as if success meant never spilling, never tripping, never saying the wrong thing.

But being human is a contact sport.

You will stumble. You will screw things up. You will cry in parking lots and laugh at wildly inappropriate times.

And guess what? That's where the magic lives.

Being a glorious disaster doesn't mean you're broken. It means you're *alive.*

You care enough to try, brave enough to risk, and humble enough to laugh when it all falls apart.

When you embrace your glorious disaster self, you stop hiding your weirdness, your flaws, your quirks — and you start realizing they're your superpowers.

Your loud laugh? *It's joy that refuses to shrink.*

Your overthinking? *It's proof that you care deeply.*

Your mistakes? *Evidence that you're showing up for your own life.*

The world doesn't need your perfection. It needs your permission — to be real.

Lessons from the Mess

Here's what the mess has taught me (usually the hard way):

Control is overrated.
The tighter you grip, the faster things slip through your fingers. Let go a little. Life isn't meant to be micromanaged.

Embarrassment is temporary; regret lasts longer.
You'll survive that awkward moment. What you won't survive is living a half-life because you were afraid to look silly.

Chaos builds character — and comedy.
Today's meltdown is tomorrow's hilarious story. (If you can laugh about it later, you're already winning.)

Growth is not tidy.
Healing doesn't happen in straight lines. Sometimes it looks like crying

in your car, then dancing in your kitchen fifteen minutes later. That's not instability — that's resilience with flair.

Love thrives in imperfection.

You don't bond with people over how perfect your life is. You bond over how spectacularly human you all are.

When I Finally Stopped Trying to Be "Fixed"

There was a time — not that long ago — when I treated self-improvement like a full-time job.

Even being on the counseling profession, I read every book, listened to every podcast, and made lists titled "New, Better Me."

Then one day, I caught myself writing "relax more" on a self-help to-do list and realized: I had officially lost the plot.

So I quit. Not on myself, but on the performance.

I stopped chasing the idea of "the healed version" of me and started showing up as *this* version — the one who still loses her patience, forgets why she walked into the kitchen, and occasionally eats ice cream for dinner (while claiming to eat healthy).

And you know what happened? Life got lighter.

I started laughing more, connecting more, *being* more.

Because fixing yourself is exhausting. But loving yourself — even in your glorious disaster state — is freeing.

Why Authentic Beats Impressive Every Time

There's something magnetic about people who are unapologetically themselves.

They're not trying to impress anyone — they're too busy being present.

Think about it: the people you love most aren't the ones with flawless homes and curated Instagram feeds.

They're the ones who hand you a mug that doesn't match, make you laugh until your stomach hurts, and make you feel safe just by being real.

Authenticity isn't flashy, but it's unforgettable.

It's what draws people to you — not because you're perfect, but because you're *approachable*.

You stop performing for approval when you realize the people who truly matter don't need a show. They just need *you*.

Practical Chaos Management - How to Function When You're a Glorious Disaster

Lower the bar.
   Seriously. You don't need a 10-step morning routine and a gratitude journal bound in moonlight. *Just breathe*. Shower. Feed yourself something vaguely nutritious. You're doing great.

Laugh first, cry later. Or vice versa.
   Either order works. Both are cleansing.

Keep a "Chaos Kit."

Mine has chocolate, a hair tie, an emergency playlist, and a friend I can text "Send memes immediately," and a bottle of wine that can be opened at a moment's notice.

Say "Oh well" more often.

Life's too short for overreactions. When something goes sideways, shrug and move on. There's power in the pivot.

Remember, everyone's a mess — just in different fonts.

Don't believe the branding. Every calm face you see in public has a personal blooper reel playing in private.

The Moment You Start Loving the Chaos

There's this quiet, beautiful shift that happens when you stop running from your chaos and start dancing with it.

You stop trying to "fix" everything and realize — maybe you were never broken.

You start to notice that even in the mess — especially in the mess — there's humor, connection, and beauty.

You can miss the turn, forget the milk, lose your cool, and still be entirely worthy of love and laughter.

Because being human isn't about having it all together. It's about holding it all — the joy, the fear, the uncertainty — and saying, "Yep, this is me."

The Takeaway

You are not a project to perfect.

You are a person to love — exactly as you are, coffee stains and all.

You're not behind. You're not broken. You're not supposed to look like anyone else's highlight reel.

You're just gloriously, beautifully, resiliently *you*.

And that's not something to hide — that's something to celebrate.

So go ahead — be the glorious disaster you were always meant to be.

Laugh too loud. Cry when you need to.

Spill something. Forget something. Start again.

Because the real beauty of life isn't in getting it right — it's in getting back up, grinning, and saying, "Well... that could've gone better."

6

When Perfection Goes to the Gym (and Never Leaves)

What striving to be perfect does to your body and mind — and why your nervous system needs a snack and a nap.

You know that feeling when your brain insists it's fine, but your body's quietly Googling "how to fake your own death for rest"? Yeah. That's perfectionism's favorite side effect.

Perfection doesn't just live in your head — it takes up *entire condos* in your nervous system. It's the muscle tension in your shoulders, the three-hour "why did I say that" replay at 2 a.m., and the gut feeling that your best effort was still "not enough."

If perfection had a workout routine, it would look like this:

- **Cardio:** Running through worst-case scenarios 24/7.
- **Strength Training:** Carrying guilt for things you can't control.
- **Stretching:** Bending over backward to make everyone happy.
- **Cooldown:** None. Ever.

And what do you get in return? A free membership to Burnout Bootcamp, featuring sleepless nights, stress acne, and a resting heart rate that thinks you're running from a tiger.

The Science-ish Part - (For anyone who likes data with their drama)

When you're chasing perfection, your body basically thinks you're in danger all the time. Cortisol — your stress hormone — starts throwing a rave in your bloodstream. Your muscles tense, your digestion stalls, and your brain cancels all chill-related activities.

Your inner perfectionist calls it "motivation."

Your body calls it "help."

The more you chase flawless, the more your nervous system forgets how to relax — until you're living in a perpetual "almost panic." You can't tell if you're anxious or just extremely alert about dust particles.

The Mind Games

Perfection convinces you that peace will come *after* you get everything right.

Spoiler: that line keeps moving.

You start micromanaging your own emotions like an unpaid intern. You reword texts 17 times. You "edit" your laughter when it's too loud. You try to meditate perfectly and then feel bad that your meditation wasn't peaceful enough.

Perfection tells you it's about excellence — but what it really wants is control.

And control is just fear in a business-casual outfit.

The Plot Twist: Your Body Already Knows Better

Every time you belly-laugh, dance like no one's watching, or just sit on the couch without guilt, your body goes,

"Oh thank God, we're safe."

That's your nervous system remembering what *living* feels like.

When you rest, breathe, or laugh, your parasympathetic nervous system (the chill one) finally gets to clock in. Your heartbeat slows, digestion restarts, and your brain takes off its emotional Spanx.

The Genius Move: Make Peace a Practice, Not a Prize

You don't need to earn rest, joy, or laughter by first "getting your act together."

You need them *because* you're human — and being human is messy cardio.

Perfection promises control.

Peace delivers connection.

And one of them requires a yoga mat, a spreadsheet, and a mild identity crisis.

The other just asks you to exhale.

Real Talk

Perfection is like that overachieving friend who always says,

"You could do more."

But peace — she's the one handing you coffee saying,

"You've done enough. Sit down."

Guess which one I'm inviting over from now on.

7

Forgive Yourself Already

The Shame Highlight Reel

You ever have those random flashbacks where your brain just decides to embarrass you for sport?

You'll be living your best life — driving, showering, minding your business — when suddenly your brain's like, *"Remember that thing you said in 2009 that made everyone uncomfortable?"*

It's like our minds keep a personal "Shame Highlight Reel," playing the greatest hits of every dumb decision, every failed relationship, every text we wish we could un-send.

And because our brains are jerks, they play it on loop — usually at 2:00 a.m.

We tell ourselves it's because we're being responsible adults, learning from our mistakes. But really, it's emotional self-torture disguised as reflection.

If we burned "guilt calories", we'd all have six-packs and a tight ass.

Why We Punish Ourselves

Here's the twisted logic of the human brain:

We think that if we just feel *bad enough*, we'll somehow balance the scales — that shame will make us better, cleaner, or more deserving of happiness again.

It's like we believe pain is the down payment for redemption.

But here's the truth: you can't shame yourself into healing. You can't punish yourself into peace.

You can't bully yourself into becoming the person you needed when you made that mistake.

You can, however, keep yourself stuck in the same cycle of regret until your inner critic needs a nap.

The Myth of "Deserving" Forgiveness

We love to make forgiveness conditional.

We'll say, "I'll forgive myself once I've made it right," or "once I've proven I've changed."

But that's not forgiveness. That's parole.

Forgiveness isn't about deserving — it's about deciding.

It's choosing to stop reliving the pain on repeat. It's the quiet, stubborn act of saying, *"I'm done bleeding for something that's already healed."*

And yes, you can forgive yourself before everyone else does.

Because if you wait for unanimous approval before letting go, you'll die waiting.

When I Finally Stopped Beating Myself Up

There was a period in my life when I was an Olympic-level overthinker.

If regret had a loyalty program, I'd have earned the platinum tier.

After my divorce, I spent months replaying everything — every conversation, every missed signal, every "what if" and "should have."

I thought if I could just analyze it hard enough, I'd find the exact moment everything broke and magically fix it retroactively.

I didn't.

What I did find was exhaustion.

I was tired of dragging that guilt around like an emotional carry-on bag I refused to check.

One night, I sat at my kitchen table with a glass of wine and a mountain of "what ifs," and I just said out loud, "I forgive you" to myself.

Not the big dramatic movie kind — no thunder, no enlightenment, just a tired woman talking to herself.

But I meant it.

And something inside me — that tight, clenched part that had been holding on for dear life — finally exhaled.

It wasn't about excusing anything. It was about *ending the internal war.*

The Weight of the "Unforgiven" You

Here's what no one tells you:

Every time you refuse to forgive yourself, you're carrying every past version of you on your back.
   The teenage you who didn't know better.
   The 20-something you who learned the hard way.
   The midlife you who was just trying to survive the storm.

You don't owe those versions punishment. You owe them peace.

You can't grow into who you're becoming while dragging around who you used to be.

Forgiveness doesn't erase the past — it just stops it from hijacking your present.

And let's be honest — you've suffered enough. You've done your time. You're allowed to stop being your own warden.

Guilt vs. Growth

There's a difference between accountability and self-abuse.

Guilt says, "I did something bad."

Shame says, "I *am* bad."

Growth says, "I learned something — and I'm not that person anymore."

Guilt is a compass; shame is a cage.

One helps you course-correct. The other keeps you from moving at all.

So if you're still punishing yourself for something that taught you to be kinder, wiser, or stronger — stop. The lesson's over, and you passed. That's not a failure anymore; it's proof you grew.

How to Actually Forgive Yourself (Even If You've Tried Before)

Forgiving yourself isn't a one-time event. It's a practice — and it's clumsy, like yoga for the soul.
Here's how to start:

Name It.
Don't downplay what happened. Call it what it was — not to reopen the wound, but to stop it from festering in silence.

Talk to Yourself Like a Person You Love.
You would probably never tell your best friend, "You're unforgivable, you ruined
everything, and you should feel bad forever."
So why say it to yourself?

Apologize — and Mean It.
Not performatively. Not in guilt. Just honestly: "I'm sorry I didn't know better then."
Sometimes that's all that old version of you needed to hear.

Do Something Kind.
Acts of kindness toward others (and yourself) rewrite your brain's guilt

loop.

Generosity heals. Compassion closes the gap between regret and redemption.

Burn the Damn Receipt.

Stop keeping score.

You don't need to "earn" peace by suffering longer. You've already paid your dues.

Why We Resist Forgiving Ourselves

Because letting go feels like letting ourselves off the hook.

It feels like we're saying, "What I did didn't matter."

But that's not true. Forgiveness isn't saying it didn't matter — it's saying it doesn't get to *own* you anymore.

You can honor the lesson without worshiping the wound.

You can remember without reliving.

Forgiveness isn't about rewriting the past — it's about releasing it — it's the moment you stop living under the weight of what's already over.

The Funny Thing About Freedom

Once you forgive yourself, life gets lighter — and strangely, funnier.

The same memories that used to sting, start to make you smile.

You begin to see your past self not as a villain, but as a well-meaning idiot doing their best with the tools they were given.

We all have that version — the one who thought love would fix everything, or that saying "yes" to everyone would make us more likable, or that using lemon juice as hair bleach was a good idea in 1989.

You can hate that person or you can hug them.

One will drain you. The other will heal you.

The Science of Self-Forgiveness

(Or, "Why Your Therapist Keeps Telling You to Journal About It")

When you forgive yourself, you literally change your brain chemistry.

You lower cortisol (stress), raise serotonin (calm), and open the door for creativity, empathy, and joy.

Your nervous system stops living in "fight or flight" and moves into "okay, maybe we'll survive this."

You stop being the defendant in your own mental courtroom and start being the judge who finally says, "Case closed."

Rewriting the Narrative

Think about the worst thing you've done — the one that still pops into your head uninvited.

Now reframe it.

Ask yourself:

- What did it teach me?

- How did it change the way I treat people?
- How would I handle it differently now?

That's not denial — that's evolution.

You can't hate the parts of you that taught you wisdom.

Forgiveness as a Superpower

The most magnetic people in the world aren't the ones who have it all together.

They're the ones who've fallen apart and come back softer, funnier, wiser.

They don't lead with shame — they lead with *stories*.

And you can feel it when you're around them — they're safe. They've been through the fire and stopped judging others for smelling like smoke.

That's what self-forgiveness does. It turns your scars into empathy, your cringe into comedy, your regret into wisdom.

Your Takeaway

You are not your past.

You are the person who learned from it. You've done hard things. You've made mistakes. You've survived them all.

So maybe it's time to stop apologizing for existing and start celebrating that you're still here.

Forgive yourself — not because you've earned it, but because you need it.

Because peace doesn't come from perfection — it comes from permission.

And maybe that's the real genius of screwing up:
  You get to rewrite the ending.

8

The Joy of Not Knowing What Comes Next

How to Make Peace with the Plot Twists You Didn't See Coming

The Great Cosmic Curveball

If life had a warning label, it would say:

"May cause spontaneous change of plans, unexpected emotional growth, and the occasional identity crisis."

We love the illusion of control. We plan, predict, and panic when the script doesn't follow the storyboard we drew in our heads. But life? Life's a cosmic improv show, and the universe is the comedian who thrives on unscripted moments.

You can have your vision board, your timeline, your tidy goals — and then boom: your job changes, your relationship ends, your health shifts, your best friend moves to another city, or your washing machine explodes on a Tuesday.

And the universe just shrugs, like, *"Curve Ball!"*

It's not personal. It's just proof you're alive in a story that's still being written.

The Control Myth

Control is our favorite coping mechanism.

We believe if we plan well enough, we'll avoid pain. If we prepare hard enough, we'll dodge disappointment.

So we build color-coded schedules, read productivity hacks, and keep emergency snacks in the car (just in case).

And sure, structure can be helpful — but control? Control is often fear wearing a headset. We control because we're scared of being caught off guard again.

But here's the problem: life's greatest gifts don't come on schedule.

The job you didn't get opened the door to the one that changed everything.

The relationship that ended gave you your freedom back so you could meet your true love.

The year that fell apart taught you who you really are when the pieces don't fit neatly together.

When you stop clinging to certainty, you start discovering possibility.

When the Plan Falls Apart (and So Do You)

I used to be a planner. The kind of planner who made lists for her lists.

I had timelines, goals, and backup goals.

And then life — in its usual show-stopping way — decided to test how flexible I *really* was.

Divorce wasn't part of the plan. Starting over wasn't part of the plan.

For a while, I fought it. I tried to wrestle my life back into the shape I thought it should take.

But plans are fragile things. They crumble under the weight of reality. So I learned to stop clinging and start listening.

One night, sitting on my porch with a glass of wine and zero clue what came next, I realized something important:

The plan had fallen apart — but I hadn't.

I was still here. Still breathing. Still capable of laughter, love, and new beginnings.

Sometimes "everything falling apart" is just the universe's way of saying, *"This chapter's done. Let's write a better one."*

The Gift of Not Knowing

We treat uncertainty like a threat when it's really an invitation. Not knowing what comes next means *anything* could come next.

It means you're not stuck in the same loop, not doomed to the same mistakes, not limited to what you can already imagine.

When you loosen your grip on certainty, you make room for miracles. And by "miracles," I don't mean angel choirs and golden light — I mean the small, quiet surprises that show up when you stop over-managing your own life.

The friend who calls at the right time.

The idea that drops into your head on a random walk.

The chance encounter that changes your direction of your entire future.

The unknown is uncomfortable, yes — but it's also full of *undiscovered good*.

The Fear Beneath the Fear

Most of us don't actually fear the unknown. We fear losing control.

We fear making the wrong choice, wasting time, being embarrassed, or not being able to handle what's coming.

But here's what's wild: every hard thing you've ever survived started with you *not knowing* how you'd survive it.

And yet — you did.

Uncertainty isn't the enemy. Distrust in yourself is.

The antidote to fear isn't more planning — it's more *faith*.

Faith that you'll figure it out, even if you don't have the map. Faith that chaos won't destroy you — it'll refine you.

You don't need to know what's next when you know *you*.

Trusting Yourself (Even When You Don't Have a Clue)

There's a strange comfort in realizing that your track record for surviving bad days is still at 100%.

You've been through the unexpected before — heartbreak, setbacks, detours — and here you are.

Maybe you didn't handle it gracefully. Maybe you cried in your car, or stress-cleaned your whole house, or binge-watched six hours of Netflix in emotional hibernation. Fine. You still survived it.

Trust isn't about having it all figured out. It's about knowing you'll figure it out *again*.

When you trust yourself, you don't need every answer. You just need one belief:
  I can handle whatever happens next.

Finding Joy in the Chaos

Joy doesn't come from knowing. It comes from *not needing to know.*

Think about the best moments in your life — the laughter you didn't plan, the opportunities that came out of nowhere, the love that found you when you'd given up on looking.

Those moments were surprises. They were the reward for staying open when you could've closed.

When life doesn't go according to plan, it's not a failure — it's feedback.

It's life's way of saying, "I have something better, but it's going to require a little faith and maybe a nap."

Joy lives in that space between "What now?" and "Oh... this."

How to Embrace Uncertainty Without Losing Your Mind

Here's the practical, slightly ridiculous truth: uncertainty isn't going away. So you might as well make friends with it.

Try these little tricks to ease the chaos:

Stop forecasting doom.

If your imagination is going to run wild, at least let it run toward something fun. "What if everything works out?" is just as valid as the opposite.

Find one thing that's certain right now.

Like the warmth of your coffee, the roof over your head, the friend who always texts you back, or the fact that you've survived 100% of your worst days so far.

Replace "What if?" with "Even if."

"What if I fail?" becomes "Even if I do, I'll learn something."
That small language shift changes panic into power.

Laugh when it's ridiculous.

Because it's all ridiculous. Life has no respect for our carefully laid plans — but laughter gives you back your balance.

Keep showing up.

You don't have to have the whole path mapped. Just take the next step with a little curiosity and a lot of courage.

When Life Doesn't Go to Plan (and Maybe That's the Point)

Some of the best things in my life happened after everything fell apart.

The divorce I thought would destroy me gave me back my voice.

The "failure" that embarrassed me became my favorite story to tell.

The uncertainty that terrified me became my freedom.

I used to beg the universe for clarity — now I just ask for resilience and a good sense of humor. Because the truth is, the not knowing *is* where the living happens.

Certainty is comfortable, but it's also boring.

Uncertainty? That's where growth, grace, and all the good plot twists hide.

The Takeaway

You don't need to have the next five years planned.

You don't even need to know what's happening next week.

You just need to keep showing up — curious, hopeful, and a little bit brave.

Because life isn't a test to pass or a puzzle to solve. It's a dance you learn as you go — occasionally out of rhythm, but still beautiful.

So here's to the joy of not knowing what comes next. To laughing when plans change. To trusting that if you can't see the whole picture, it's only because it's still being painted.

And to remembering this truth:

You don't have to know what's coming to know you'll be okay.

9

The Art of Helping Others Be Imperfect

How to Show Up Without Fixing, Save Without Saving, and Love Without Editing

How to Stop Trying to Save People Who Don't Need Saving

It starts with good intentions.

You see someone you care about struggling and you think, *"I can help."*

Next thing you know, you're knee-deep in someone else's chaos, giving advice they didn't ask for, Googling self-help quotes, and texting follow-ups like you're running a motivational hotline.

Meanwhile, they're overwhelmed, you're exhausted, and neither of you feels better.

Here's the truth no one tells you about helping people:

Most of the time, they don't need you to fix them. *They just need to know they're not broken.*

Why We Try to Fix Everyone

We try to fix people because it makes *us* feel safe.

If we can patch their pain, we don't have to face our own helplessness.

If we can solve their problems, maybe we won't have to sit in the discomfort of not having the answers.

But helping from fear isn't love — it's control in a friendlier outfit.

Sometimes the kindest thing you can do for someone isn't to give them advice — it's to give them space. To say, *"I see you, I love you, and I trust you to find your way."*

When we stop treating people like projects and start treating them like people, connection replaces correction.

What People Actually Need: Presence, Not Perfection

You don't have to have the right words. You don't have to know what to say or how to fix it.

Sometimes you just need to show up with coffee (or adult beverages) and silence.

Presence says, *"You don't have to be okay for me to love you."*

Perfection says, *"Please get okay quickly, because this is uncomfortable."*

The people who've helped me the most weren't the ones who had the best advice. They were the ones who sat next to me in my mess without judgment — who didn't rush me, who let me cry, who made me laugh in the middle of the wreckage.

They didn't tidy up my pain; they just made it feel less lonely.

That's what real compassion looks like — not solving, not fixing, just standing beside someone long enough for them to remember they're strong.

The Myth of "Good Advice"

Advice is like salt — a little bit can make things better, but too much ruins the soup.

We think if we say the perfect thing, we'll spark their breakthrough. But advice often says more about *our need to help* than their need to heal.

The truth is, people rarely remember the advice. They remember how you made them feel.

So instead of trying to give the perfect words, try giving *presence*.

Instead of thinking, "What should I say?", ask, "How can I listen?"

Being the Example, Not the Expert

You don't inspire people by looking flawless. You inspire them by being honest.

When you share your imperfections, your failures, and your "me too" moments, you create a safe space for others to do the same.

When you say, *"I've been there — and I'm still figuring it out,"* you're giving someone else permission to breathe.

Your vulnerability doesn't make you less credible — it makes you *relatable.*

We're drawn to people who are real, not people who are rehearsed.

You don't have to be the expert on imperfection. Just be the example.

The Ripple Effect of Realness

When you show up real, you give others permission to drop their masks too.

It's contagious — in the best way.

You laugh at yourself, and someone else laughs with you. You admit you don't have it all together, and suddenly no one else feels like they have to pretend either.

It's like emotional dominoes — one honest confession and the whole room exhales.

That's how we change things. Not through lectures, but through lived example.

You can't preach authenticity while editing yourself to look perfect.

You can't teach vulnerability while hiding your scars.

But when you live your truth — flaws, failures, and all — people feel it.

They trust you. They soften.

They start to believe that maybe they're okay, too.

How to Be There Without Losing Yourself

Let's be real — being supportive doesn't mean becoming someone's emotional mop.

You can be compassionate *and* have boundaries. You can care deeply without collapsing under someone else's chaos.
Here's how:

Don't over-identify.
Their story isn't your story. You can relate without carrying it.

Listen more than you advise.
Sometimes the best "help" is a quiet nod and a "Yeah, that sucks."

Ask before you advise.
"Do you want me to just listen, or do you want my opinion?"
That one sentence will save 90% of your friendships.

Take off the superhero cape.
You're a human, not a fixer. Their healing isn't your homework.

Share the real, not the rehearsed.
Sometimes the most healing thing you can say is, "I've messed that up too."

When You Want to Help But Feel Helpless

There will be moments when someone you love is hurting and there's absolutely nothing you can do. And that's the hardest part — the sitting in the helplessness.

But your love isn't measured by how many problems you solve. It's measured by your willingness to stay when it's uncomfortable.

You don't have to say the perfect thing. You just have to stay.

Love doesn't always sound like advice — sometimes it just sounds like, *"I'm here."*

Teaching Imperfection by Living It

The world doesn't need more motivational speakers. It needs more honest humans.

So teach imperfection the way it's meant to be taught — through laughter, humility, and example.

- Burn the dinner but serve it anyway.
- Admit when you're wrong without the 12-point apology.
- Let your kids see you mess up and make it right.
- Let your friends see you without makeup, metaphorical or literal.

Because when you let people see your unpolished sides, you give them permission to stop hiding theirs.

That's the art of helping others be imperfect — you don't fix them, you *free* them.

The Gift of Shared Humanity

When you stop performing perfection, you create space for others to be real.

And in that space, connection thrives.

That's where real friendship lives — in the laughter between confessions, in the *"I screwed up too"* moments that dissolve shame.

We're all just walking each other home through the chaos. No one has the map. But we do have each other.

And that's enough.

Practical Ways to Help Others Embrace Imperfection

Model it.
Be the first one to admit, "I messed that up." It lowers the temperature in every room.

Normalize failure.
Tell your stories. Share the behind-the-scenes, not just the highlight reel.

Respond to vulnerability with kindness.
When someone admits they're struggling, resist the urge to fix it — just thank them for trusting you.

Celebrate progress, not perfection.
Remind people that baby steps count. That showing up counts. That surviving the week counts.

Laugh often — especially at yourself.
Humor builds bridges where advice builds walls.

When You Lead with Compassion

People don't remember what you said or did as much as how you made them feel safe enough to be real.

Leading with compassion doesn't mean you have to carry everyone's load — it just means you help them see that theirs is carryable.

Every time you choose honesty over image, kindness over cleverness, grace over judgment — you're teaching the art of imperfection.

Not by preaching. By *being*.

The Takeaway

The best kind of help isn't heroic — it's human.

You don't need to fix anyone to change their life. You just need to show up — flawed, funny, and fully present.

When you let people see you stumble and keep going, they learn it's safe to do the same.

When you choose real over perfect, you give them permission to breathe again.
   So help softly.
   Love loudly.
   Laugh often.

Because when you show up real, you remind everyone around you that they can, too.

10

The Genius of a Gloriously Imperfect Life

How to Keep Laughing, Living, and Letting Life Be What It Is

The End (Sort Of)

You made it.

Not to the end of your problems, or your growth, or your beautifully messy journey — just to the end of this book.

If you've laughed, cried, or nodded at least once while muttering, *"Oh my God, same,"* then congratulations: you've already graduated from the school of Trying Too Hard.

You've learned that failure doesn't define you, perfection doesn't save you, and uncertainty isn't the enemy — it's the adventure.

You've learned that the point was never to have it all together. It was to stay soft enough to fall apart and strong enough to rebuild.

And that, my friend, is genius.

The Myth of "Arriving"

We spend our lives chasing the imaginary finish line where everything finally makes sense. Where we're fit, happy, successful, healed, and at peace — all at the same time, in matching loungewear.

But here's the secret no one tells you: there's no finish line.

Just a bunch of weird, wonderful pit stops where you catch your breath, learn something new, and keep going.

The goal isn't to *arrive*. The goal is to *be alive*.

You're supposed to keep evolving, keep getting it wrong, keep surprising yourself.

You're supposed to live, not just perform being okay.

Life as a Practice, Not a Performance

Somewhere along the way, we turned "self-improvement" into another contest.

We try to meditate perfectly, heal efficiently, manifest responsibly.

But life isn't a performance. It's a practice — one you'll never master, and that's kind of the point.
   The practice of laughing when things go sideways.
   The practice of forgiving faster.
   The practice of saying, "Yeah, I don't know," and not making it mean failure.
   The practice of showing up anyway.

You don't need to fix every flaw. You just need to keep practicing being human.

The Beauty of the Ordinary

Perfection sells — but real life is found in the ordinary moments:
The coffee that's slightly too cold but still comforting.
The friend who texts you a meme when words won't do.
The quiet relief of realizing that nobody's watching as closely as you think.

Genius isn't about brilliance or achievement — it's about awareness. It's noticing the joy hiding in the mess, the humor in the heartbreak, the peace in the pause.

You don't need a grand revelation. Sometimes the most profound wisdom is just, *"I'm okay right now."*

On Loving the Process

We love results. We're obsessed with outcomes — the before-and-after, the transformation, the success story.

But the process? The in-between? That's where the magic actually happens.
The days when you try and fail and try again.
The conversations that change you in small, unplanned ways.
The moments when you choose grace over guilt, laughter over shame.

That's where growth lives — in the process.

And the process is never tidy, but it's always worth it.

Your Inner Genius (Yes, You Have One)

You might not have a PhD, a viral TED Talk, or a perfect morning routine — but you have something better.

You have resilience, humor, and a ridiculous ability to keep going even when you're sure you can't.

You have a brain that overthinks, a heart that feels too much, and a spirit that refuses to quit. And somehow, that combination keeps turning chaos into character.

You don't need to be a genius *at* anything.

You just need to be a genius *at being you.*

Your Permission Slip to Be Human

So here it is — your official permission slip:

- You are allowed to screw up.
- You are allowed to change your mind.
- You are allowed to take breaks.
- You are allowed to not know.
- You are allowed to be proud of progress that no one else can see.

You're even allowed to have days where you do absolutely nothing productive — and still call it healing.

You don't owe anyone a perfect version of yourself.

You just owe yourself your own version of human.

The Ripple Effect

When you choose to be real, you give everyone around you permission to do the same.

When you laugh at your own chaos, it becomes a shared joke instead of a secret shame.

When you show kindness to yourself, it teaches others how to do it, too.

That's how the world changes — not through perfect people, but through honest ones.

Through humans who show up flawed, funny, and still full of love.

What Comes Next

I wish I could tell you that everything gets easier from here. But it doesn't — and honestly, that's good news.

Because the messy parts are where you'll find meaning.

The unexpected turns are where you'll find growth.

And the days you feel completely lost? Those are usually the ones that change you most.

You don't need certainty to have peace. You just need the courage to keep showing up.

Final Thoughts

If you take nothing else from this book, take this:

You're not a failure for falling apart.

You're not behind.

You're not too late or too much or too anything.

You're a living, breathing work in progress — and that's the best kind.

The real genius isn't in getting life right. It's in loving yourself when you don't.

So go ahead — screw up like a genius.

Laugh when you can, cry when you need to, forgive yourself daily, and keep showing up for this wildly unpredictable story you're in.

Let it be imperfect. Let it be real. Let it be yours.

Afterword

First of all — thank you. Not just for reading my words, but for *staying with yourself* while you did.

Because this wasn't a book about fixing who you are — it was about finding the courage to stop pretending you're broken.

If any part of these pages made you laugh at your own chaos, forgive your past self, or breathe a little easier about the future, then I wrote it for you.

You are living proof that we don't need to be perfect to be powerful — or even remotely qualified to share what we've learned. We just need to be honest enough to say, "Yep, I screwed that up too."

I've spent enough time chasing flawless to know it doesn't exist. What does exist are moments — the kind that surprise you, soften you, and make you laugh when life clearly didn't go to plan.

So my hope for you is simple:
   That you keep showing up for your life, even when it's messy.
   That you keep forgiving the past version of you who didn't know what you know now.
   That you give yourself permission to laugh, rest, and start again — as many times as you need.

And most of all, that you keep choosing *real* over *perfect*, again and again.

Because *real* is where the good stuff lives.

Thank you for spending your time, your heart, and your quiet moments with me.

Until then — keep being gloriously, ridiculously, unapologetically human. It's the smartest thing you'll ever do.

With gratitude and grace,

L.S. Smith

The Genius Toolkit

Exercises and Reflections for

Real-Life Imperfection

*Because sometimes you need more than
inspiration — you need a nudge, a notebook,
and a little honesty.*

Self Forgiveness

Exercise 1

The "I Forgive You" Letter

(to Yourself)

Write a letter to yourself — not the current you, but the version of you who made that mistake, stayed too long, or didn't know better.
Be specific. Be kind. You don't need to justify — **just forgive**.

End your letter with:

"You were doing the best you could with what you had. And I love you for that."

Optional: Burn it, shred it, or fold it into a paper airplane and throw it dramatically — whatever feels right.

Exercise 2

The Self-Compassion Reframe

Grab a piece of paper.
Draw two columns:

What I Usually Tell <u>Myself</u>	What I Could Tell <u>Myself</u> Instead
"I messed everything up."	"I'm learning. This is progress in disguise."
"I should've known better."	"I didn't, and now I do — that's growth."
"I'm so behind."	"I'm right on time for *my* story."

Add your own. Then practice reading the right-hand column out loud — daily.

Exercise 3

The Mirror Apology

Stand in front of a mirror.

(yes, even if it feels weird)

Say:

"I forgive you. I release you. You don't have to keep proving your worth. You already are enough."
If you laugh halfway through, perfect. That means you're human.

Letting Go of the Past

Exercise 4

The "What Stayed" List

Instead of listing everything you lost, write what **stayed**.

What parts of you survived the hard thing?

What wisdom, strength, or humor came out of it?

That's your inventory of resilience.

Exercise 5

The "Could Have" Funeral

Write down all your "could have," "should have," and "if only" statements.

Then fold the paper and say:

"Thank you for teaching me. You're free to go."

Toss it (responsibly). That chapter is done — the new one's better.

Everyday Imperfection
Practice

Exercise 6

The Messy Gratitude List

Forget perfect gratitude journals.

Write down three things you're grateful for *that **<u>aren't</u>** Instagram-worthy.*

Example: "My favorite mug survived the dishwasher," or "My boss didn't schedule a 4 p.m. meeting."

Gratitude doesn't need glitter — it needs honesty.

Repeat daily or weekly (whenever you can spare the time)

You will become grateful for the small things in life.

Exercise 7

The Real Talk Check-In

At the end of your day, ask yourself:

- Did I speak kindly to myself today?

- Did I let something be imperfect?

- Did I laugh?

If you answered "no" to any of these, you get to try again tomorrow.

Exercise 8

The "Show Up Anyway" Promise

Write this at the top of a page (or your mirror):

"I will keep showing up, even when it's awkward, uncertain, or messy — because that's where life actually happens."

Sign it. Date it.

You're officially licensed to be human.

Helping Others Heal
Imperfectly

Exercise 9

The Listening Pledge

Next time a friend vents, resist the urge to give advice.

Instead, say:

"That sounds tough. Do you want me to listen or brainstorm with you?"

You'll be amazed how much peace that one sentence brings.

Exercise 10

The "Real Connection" Challenge

Go one full day without pretending everything's fine.

When someone asks, "How are you?" — answer honestly, even if it's, "Honestly? A little tired but hanging in there."

Authenticity breeds authenticity.

The Forgiveness Manifesto

Finish this statement in your own words:

"From now on, I will forgive myself for..."

Write until you run out of things to write. Then read it back — and notice how much lighter it feels to see the truth on paper.

✦ Ten Genius Truths to Keep Handy ✦

1. Perfection is exhausting. Progress is where the peace is.

2. You can't heal by hating who you were. Forgive yourself. That version got you here.

3. Laughter counts as self-care. So does doing absolutely nothing.

4. Growth is messy. That's how you know it's real.

5. You don't need to have it all together. You just need to keep showing up.

6. Failure isn't the opposite of success — it's the evidence you're trying.

7. You can't control the plot twists, but you can choose your response — preferably with humor.

8. You don't need to fix everyone. Just love them where they are.

9. Peace starts when pretending ends.

10. You are allowed to be both a masterpiece and a work in progress.

"You can't carry peace and perfection in the same hands. Let it go, forgive and love your true self"

-L.S. Smith

www.ingramcontent.com/pod-product-compliance
Lightning Source LLC
Chambersburg PA
CBHW051638120626
46551CB00014B/2125